walking on snow

– the first steps

A Comprehensive Introduction to Classic Cross Country Skiing

by Keith Richardson

Contents

Chapter 3 **Practical section**

With thanks to the following individuals for their support in this project:

Erik Rustad of Rustad Hotel
Trond Lunde of Sjusjøen Fritid
Ole Berg of Nedre Berg Gård
Anders Friis of Nordseter Aktivitetssenter
Terje Dahlen of Dahlen Husky
Lars Hanstad of Madshus
Geir Kollstrøm of Lillehammer Turist
Trude Arnesen of Maihaugen
Thor Willy Christiansen of Swix
Jeanne Richardson

Foreword

If you try to read this booklet like a novel, the overwhelming amount of theory will probably give you a headache. The 'technical' and 'practical' sections could perhaps wait until you are nearly on skis, so that you can apply what you read. The intention behind this whole project is to encourage everyone and anyone to seriously consider spending a week away from noise and stress, taking gentle exercise in bright light and clean air.

Introduction

This booklet is about removing the mysteries that seem to surround cross-country skiing in the minds of people from milder climates. Questions like; would it suit me? How fit should I be? What should I take with me? How difficult is it to learn? Do I need ski-school?

You will find answers to all those questions in the following pages, but the 'would it suit me' is worth looking at right away. Having helped hundreds of beginners, I feel qualified to make a few generalisations.

Small children, up to 7 or 8yrs old, find it very hard to work for absolutely no point except to accommodate their parents. They love to play in the snow of course, but even 1km on skis can seem like a lifetime sentence – especially if you point to a distant hill and say "that is where we are going!" From 8 to 13, kids have enough muscle and energy to go like the clappers for a while, but enough is enough. The whole thing is a bit tame, saved by the occasional downhill stretch, which is definitely 'wicked'. 95% of teenagers are far happier on downhill skis or snowboards. Mutiny is very common in Norwegian families. Young couples need to be aware that toddlers under 2yrs should not spend hours at a time in a backpack or in a 'pulk' (a kind of sled). For everyone else, it is hard to guess who will take to it and who will not. There is no upper age limit, although sound lungs and heart are a considerable advantage. Many x-country skiers tend to enjoy a quiet evening around the fire with a good book or a game of scrabble. 'Knit-chicks' have always been cool in x-country circles. Endurance athletes will think they are in heaven; there is no limit to the amount of pain you can inflict on yourself if you are that way inclined. If you see someone belting along wearing a lycra suit with legs up to their armpits, they are either a competitor in training or a German tourist on holiday. Alpine skiers who are beginning to creak a bit will find that the knees, thighs and back take less punishment. In fact, x-country often positively helps with old injuries.

If you look at a snow-covered hillside and find yourself planning where and when to make your turns, then you are probably still a downhill skier at heart. You might well consider the gently undulating terrain of the x-country skier a severe waste of good snow. Every minute of time spent on x-country skis while the lifts are open will feel like wasted proper ski time. You could test this theory by hiring x-country kit for half a day next time you go to the Alps. In fact, to be fair, we are seeing long-term down hillers who are beginning to ache a bit turning to a more mixed winter holiday. A blend of activities including dog sledding, horse riding, snowshoeing and of course various sorts of skiing, seems to have growing appeal. Dahlen Husky is run by Terje (pronounced terrier), and he brings his 30+ dogs to the area on a regular basis. By common consent, this is a must. Alpine skiers will definitely notice the lack of noise and bustle in an x-country area. There are no lifts so there is no need to congregate at any one spot. The equipment is light, comfortable and easy to carry. You will find that you can relax more easily and be more aware of your surroundings. What you lose in excitement you will gain in a feeling of wellbeing. One can think of x-country as hill walking with a skill element, but not necessarily with the hills, and it is not really walking either, but we shall get to that later.

Chapter 1

Information section

Using this booklet

It would be a good idea to dip into this booklet before you have even had a pair of skis on your feet. You will get an overall feel for the sport, and hopefully realise that anyone of any age and level of fitness can enjoy the experience, whether walking quietly over the winter landscape or testing your endurance to the limit. You can get started with professional help, or just have a go and pick things up along the way. I would recommend that you have formal tuition for at least the first two hours, if only to help with confidence and to find out exactly what you need to practice in your own time. Either way, this book is designed to help. There is a huge amount of information in these pages, and much of it will not make much sense until you have done at least a few hours skiing. If you reread sections as you gain experience, more of the subtleties will become clear. There will come a point when you will have technical questions that are not covered here, but by then you will have mastered the basics and have progressed beyond the scope of the booklet.

I have become very familiar with the area around Lillehammer in Norway, so although there are numerous references to times of day, seasons and so on wich are particularly relevant to this environment, the information is largely applicable wherever you choose to go skiing.

Maihaugen

THE OPEN AIR MUSEUM tells us about living and working in Norway over the course of 500 years. The houses and people provide a framework that makes a visit to MAIHAUGEN a journey through time.

OPENING HOURS
1. OCT - 17 MAY 11.00 - 16.00
MONDAYS CLOSED.

MAIHAUGEN

Maihaugveien 1
2609 Lillehammer
Norway
Tel. +47 61 28 89 00
Fax +47 61 28 89 01
www.maihaugen.no

A visit to Maihaugen is one of the worthwhile alternatives to skiing. This is both an indoor and outdoor sampling of ancient and modern Norway, and it will take a few hours to do it justice. The point is that even though you are on a ski holiday, it is advisable to break up the week to allow the body to recuperate.

Bars of soap

For those readers who have never done any 'slippery' sports such as skateboarding, skating, roller-skating or water skiing, the following analogy could help you to understand the concept of x-country skiing.

Imagine that you are standing on two large bars of soap, one under each foot, on a wet lino floor. I say imagine because I don't recommend that you try it. Now, in order to cross the room, you would have to shuffle with small steps and you would make it, but you must agree that sounds pretty inefficient. If there was a way to get some momentum going, you could just stand there while the soap slid across the floor, with you going for the ride. That would require some balance, but would be much less work. Let us suppose that there was just enough friction between the soap and the floor that you were able to push off with one foot and balance on the other as you launch yourself across the floor. You could travel relatively large distances, with an occasional new launch to keep the momentum going. If you were to lift your front foot even slightly, you would of course lose the soap. The tricky part is to balance precisely over the moving bar of soap. It actually doesn't take too long to get the idea, and besides, skis are nowhere near as treacherous as soap.

Let this be a warning shot across the bows of alpine skiers, they can get away with terrible balance because of their massive boots and big, fat skis, and besides, they are more or less balancing over both skis most of the time, giving a much bigger platform to stand on. It is a bit of a mystery why x-country has been kept a virtual secret from the British skier, when you consider how many of us enjoy walking, jogging, cycling, rambling and just working out. I suspect it is an image problem. As a young alpine skier some 35yrs ago, I would rather have cut my arm off than put on a pair of x-country skis. Now I groan inwardly if I am faced with a day in Alpine boots. True, there is less excitement in my life these days, but there is just as much fun.

Tracks

X-country skiing has evolved into two quite separate disciplines. Below is a chance meeting of two 'classic' skiers who are each sliding along in a pair of ruts or grooves which have been cut by a special attachment fixed to the back of a heavy snowcat. Where there are two tracks, one generally uses the track on the right. It is quite normal to occupy both tracks when skiing with a friend, but the person on the left should always give way to oncoming traffic. Narrow tracks through woods etc. are often laid by a snow scooter or even cut by the skiers themselves. Good manners and common sense should sort out priority. The wide flat area between two sets of tracks can be used by classic skiers, but is really the domain of the 'skaters'. Skating is a relatively recent form of skiing and has become an Olympic sport in it's own right. Tracks are groomed regularly because they are quickly destroyed by wind, new snow, sun or simply through use. Newly cut tracks are easier to ski in, badly worn ones can be quite unpleasant.

Winter or spring?

It is a sad fact that sun is bad for snow. In the depths of winter, new snow is usually soft, dry and powdery. The temperature stays below zero for many weeks, and because there is very little power in the sun, snow does not melt enough to form a crust. It is not usually possible to make a snowman or even a snowball until spring! Winter snow allows the skis to glide smoothly and quietly, makes waxing easy, looks beautiful and is lovely and soft to fall on, should you require that facility. When the temperature is between -3 and -12, it is cool enough to keep the snow in good condition and warm enough to enjoy a whole day's skiing in comfort. I kid thee not, the air is so dry that those temperatures do not make you feel cold provided you are wearing appropriate clothing and don't stand around for ages. It is humidity rather than temperature that makes you shiver.

Later in the year, from late March onwards, the snow becomes distinctly less friendly. Heat from the sun causes free water to appear in the snow crystals, which changes their characteristics completely. Now the ski tracks become firm if not icy, freezing every night and softening up slowly during the morning. Not even the track making machines can do much about the ice. They do grind it up a bit, but they leave fist-sized lumps of rock hard snow, affectionately known as 'death cookies'. By about 11.00am on a sunny spring morning the south facing tracks are soft enough to take beginners on. The bonus of warmer weather is that one can ski for a while and then sit and enjoy a leisurely picnic in total peace and quiet.

You can be unlucky with the weather of course, but this area of Norway is renowned for it's stable climate. It is almost never too windy to ski, it doesn't rain from Nov until April, a cold snap rarely lasts more than 3 or 4 days and even then the sky is usually a clear brilliant blue. We get about 4 to 6ft of snow, which sounds a lot, but that represents only 6 to 7in of rain. The snow that falls does not melt, so by Dec. there is always skiing to be had, and it just gets better. There is little to compare with the pleasure of meandering quietly between snow-covered trees on a carpet of pristine, glittering snow. The tourist office at Lillehammer has a much visited website, and the office itself is situated at the train station, which is where you will arrive if you used the direct line from under Gardemoen airport.

Excellent variation

for more information visit **www.lillehammerturist.no**

B.A.S.I. manual

The long awaited BASI Nordic Manual (British Association of Snowsport Instructors) is now available, and is an in-depth look at both classic and skating techniques. It is aimed at the more advanced skier who hopes to become an instructor, or to anyone who wants to improve their understanding of skiing. That manual would be a natural progression for the reader, for it goes well beyond the scope of this booklet.

This is one of those lycra suits I mentioned. If you do have the nerve (and the figure) to wear one of these slinky numbers, you have to go like a train just to keep warm. These boys and girls are lungs on legs and ski huge distances just for the fun of it. Hobbies: marathon running and sleeping on nails.

Hiring equipment

When you have settled in and unpacked, you might have time to sort out the equipment you need. I strongly suggest that you don't bother bringing skis etc. with you until you have some experience. Ski-hire shops these days offer more than adequate equipment, advice and servicing. It does not always work to bring, say, a pair of boots that you have tried on at home. The boots may not be compatible with the hire skis, or they maybe feel wrong when actually skiing. Much easier to hire everything and change stuff as and when. Those who travel by air, even if they come every year, will tend to hire to keep life simple. Trond runs Sjusjøen (pronounced shoe-shurn) Fritid, which is the friendliest hire shop you will ever find, situated up near the supermarket. If you are staying at Nordseter, then Anders Friis and co. have a bit of an empire with café, ski hire and cabins for hire.

"I'm sorry sir, but I can't make this boot fit onto those skis."

SJUSJØEN FRITID
2612 SJUSJØEN

- Skirental

- Sport - shop

- Ski instruction

- Activities

info@sjusjoen-fritid.no
www.sjusjoen-fritid.no

Skirental - Skischool - Skishop
Café - Activities

The best place for Nordic Skiing!

www.nordseter.no

Cabins (5-24 persons)
Appartments (3-15 persons)

Nordsetervegen 1303
2618 Lillehammer
Norway

Tel   +47 61 26 40 12
Fax +47 61 26 40 88
booking@nordseter.no

Boots

Go for comfort. There are many makes and styles, so keep trying different ones until you find some that fit like slippers. The toes should not reach the end, nor should the heel lift more than a very small amount. When you bend your foot as far as you can, the boot will of course ruck up across the toes. If there is a ridge pressing against your toes in the wrong spot, it can get pretty sore after a while, so change them sooner rather than later. Your toes should not be cramped at all, that causes poor circulation, which will lead to cold feet. Blisters should be a thing of the past, but invest in a plaster and change the boots anyway. One pair of good quality thermal socks is adequate down to about -12c because the boots are insulated to a degree.

Skis

The hire shop should know exactly which pair to give you. Just tell them you are a beginner and trust that they give you the appropriate stiffness and length of ski. All that really matters is that the binding works properly and that the base of the ski is ready for waxing. They should not give you a pair of skis with the previous user's wax on them, unless it happens to be the right wax for that day. Not all bindings are compatible with all boots, so if you ask to be shown how to connect your boots to the skis, you will see how they work and if they work!

Poles

Life will be much easier if your poles are the right length. They should reach from the ground to your armpit. There will be a plastic basket on the sharp end to stop the pole from digging into the snow too far, and some form of strap on each handle. These straps will probably need adjusting, so again, ask how to do that for there are several systems on the market. Ideally, there should be about 2cm of handle sticking out above your gloved hand when the straps are correctly adjusted. The poles are very light and tend to take some punishment, so it is quite normal to be handed a pair that is slightly bent. They can usually be straightened over a knee.

Protection

Some people who are trying x-country for the first time have never experienced full winter before. There is nothing quite like first hand experience, but a few tips might be in order, to help you to work out what to bring with you.

Sun

Even in January, there is quite a lot of ultraviolet about because what little gets through the atmosphere bounces off the snow, increasing the amount you absorb. Don't be fooled by cloud cover, it still gets through. As a rule of thumb, you should wear sunglasses if you find you are squinting or if you can feel the heat of the sun on your face. If in doubt wear eye protection because snow blindness is extremely unpleasant. Sun, wind and cold can all affect sensitive skin, and when you have all three together, even leathery old diehards will feel the effects. A medium sun block, particularly on the nose, should do the job. One more thing about the sun; when it goes down, so does the temperature, and quickly too.

Wind

For every 2km per hr. of wind speed, the effective temperature against the body falls by 1c. On windy days, it can feel much warmer amongst the trees. An exposed track can become quite an experience. The wind can obliterate a track in minutes, snow driven horizontally will reduce visibility drastically and the continual buffeting is exhausting. A headwind makes for heavy going and a side-wind will freeze half of your face, so when planning a tour on a windy day, try to cross any exposed terrain with the wind at your back. Trees make a wonderful windbreak.

Cold

There is cold and there is too cold. Too cold starts at -25c and just gets worse. Not much fun to be out more than a few minutes at a time. A word of warning about that old cliché of sticking to things: it is absolutely true. If you have a slightly sweaty hand and you take off your glove to touch something metal when the temperature is around -20 or colder, you will stick to it. Don't panic, because you will leave skin behind if you try to pull your hand away. A cup of warm water or whatever poured slowly over the contact point will immediately heat the metal enough to free the hand. I had a Welsh fusilier stuck by his tongue to a chairlift because he felt compelled to test the theory. It is amazing how far a tongue will stretch if the owner panics enough.

Frost bite

Everyone has heard horror stories about climbers and explorers suffering tremendous hardship with exposure, frostbite and the like. For them, it is part of the challenge. You, on the other hand, will never be far from shelter and other skiers when on a ski holiday, so even if things go wrong, help is available long before you are in serious trouble. Frost-nip, however, is something to be aware of. When fingers or toes begin to hurt, you should take steps to warm them up; more protection, find a café or ski a bit harder for a while. Cheeks, ears and nose might well turn white without hurting, so in low temperatures one should keep an eye on fellow skiers, particularly children. A body part that has turned white and feels numb has frozen. This is absolutely not serious, and gentle heat such as a warm hand or simply going indoors for a few minutes will restore circulation. Things can sting a bit when the blood flows again, but it soon goes over. The big no-no is to ignore painfully cold fingers or toes; when they stop hurting, they have frozen and are one step closer to frostbite. Permanent damage becomes a possibility.

Clothing

They say over here that there is no such thing as bad weather, only bad clothing. Actually that is not too far from the truth. The whole idea when skiing is to wear, or have with you, whatever clothing will keep you at a comfortable temperature. Getting wet from the inside is of much greater concern than from the outside. Rainwear is rarely needed, even in late spring, and snow simply brushes off. A typical outer layer is wind-proof and breathable, but not particularly waterproof. Alpine skiers bring their one-piece or two-piece suits with them, and these work very well for beginners when it is cold, but are too warm to use on all but the most gentle of outings. The basic principle of effective clothing is that one should wear several thin layers rather than rely on a bulky outer layer. Next to your skin should be a thermal material, such as polypropylene, that is capable of removing or absorbing moisture from the body. A pair of alpine type trousers would then be more than adequate for the lower half. The top half, particularly the trunk, needs more layers. Start the day with too much on, you can always remove layers which you might well be glad of later in the day. Over the thermals could go a polo-neck, followed by a fleece or wool sweater. The outer layer should be wind-proof in this particular case, as much to allow the various under layers to hold their warmth as to keep out the wind. It would be a mistake to wear any clothing that was unable to breathe when you are taking exercise. Wool socks are hard to beat for warmth, but they can itch, so a thin pair of those expensive jobs that you see in designer packets in sport shops, make a big difference to comfort and warmth, when worn as a first layer. Cotton socks are adequate in the spring, but not when it is cold. A wool/acrylic/cotton mix would be better. Gloves need to keep your fingers warm, especially if it is windy, but most of the time thick gloves are too warm. One option is to slip a pair of gauntlets over regular windproof gloves, but some people prefer to wear thermal inner gloves with substantial gortex outers. A warm hat is an essential because so much of the body's heat is lost through the head, but that said, removing one's hat is an excellent way of regulating the body's temperature. Ears need covering in cold weather or wind, and the neck should be protected by at least something that can be zipped up if needed.

Fuel

Endurance athletes know all about what and when to eat and drink when taking exercise. For most of us, a week of walking around in the snow is a lot more than we normally would do. When a novice to x-country skiing suddenly and inexplicably runs out of energy, nine times out of ten the reason is that they got their liquid intake wrong. The air in winter is pretty dry, you use up energy just keeping warm, and you are taking exercise and using nervous energy while becoming familiar with the sport. Even though you may not feel sweaty, you can be sure that you are losing moisture at a much faster rate than usual. Always take something to drink if you plan to be out for more than a couple of hours. A thermos of hot solbaer (Ribena) is traditional here when it is cold, but chocolate, coffee or tea is better than nothing. In warm weather, one should drink little and often, perhaps a couple of mouthfuls every time you stop.

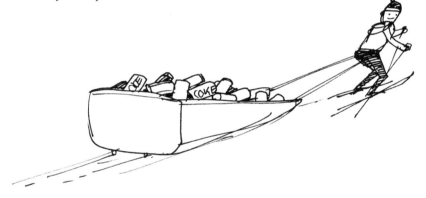

I was quizzing a customer, who happened to be a kidney specialist from Israel, for information about drinks of various sorts. I was surprised to hear that Coke is one of the best liquids for replacing electrolytes and generally revitalising the body. I looked up the Coke website some time later, but could find nothing specific either way. Alcohol, on the other hand, is not very compatible with this sport, although 'a little of what you fancy does you good'. One useful tip is that if your urine is strongly coloured, it can mean that your kidneys are probably in good working order, but they could do with a bit more liquid in the system. Food is not nearly so important as drink for recreational skiers, even though you will doubtless develop a healthy appetite, but don't think you can have a green light on chocolate. The body does not readily absorb the fats in chocolate during exercise. Sorry about that.

Backpack

All potential disasters can be minimised by using a bit of common sense and by carrying a backpack containing a few essentials. For your first few days of skiing, all you need is something to drink, over-gloves or warm gloves, a map, possibly a compass, a couple of waxes and a cork, a spare pair of socks and a wind-proof top if you don't start with one on. A nice addition would be a mobile phone with your hotel number logged in. The pack should be large enough to hold any clothes you might be removing during the day. In springtime, a full picnic and something to sit on become essentials!

Boots on ice

They say that if you no longer fall over when walking on ice, then you have been here too long. Ordinary boots are bad enough, but ski boots are not designed for walking in. When you have to walk along a road or track, try to stay on the rough parts and avoid smooth ice whenever possible. If you slip, it is usually the front foot that has shot out in front of you, and you go over backwards. To avoid falling, it will help to use one or both ski poles for balance, and take shorter steps, placing each foot flat rather than heel first. That way you can cross over icy patches without further denting your dignity.

A day trip

The trick here is to keep an eye on the time rather than the distance. Start by deciding how many hours you want to be out for. As a beginner, you can reckon on skiing at about 3km per hour, roughly the same as slow walking speed. If you are a sporty type, you could easily double that. Always build in a generous safety margin in the early days, as there are bound to be unexpected delays or slow progress for a variety of reasons. It is good policy to café-hop. Try to plan your route to take in as many resting places as possible until you get to know the terrain and your own limitations. If you find yourself less than half way round your planned route, and you have used up half the time available, then you should either take a short cut you are sure of or turn back. Mountain weather can change quickly and dramatically. It can be very difficult to find people in a blizzard, so don't take risks until you have enough experience to know how much of a risk you are taking. You will enjoy your holiday more if you pace yourself cleverly and take lots of breaks along the way.

Chapter 2

Technical section

Ski design

Recreational track skis are usually straight, narrower than your boots and taper at both ends. The tip is pointed and turned up to stop it digging into the snow. A groove runs down the centre of the base to help keep it tracking in a straight line. Most inexpensive skis are made largely of wood with other materials laminated on and under for increased performance and cosmetic reasons. There is a single binding, mounted centrally on the ski, designed to accept the toe bar on a ski boot. A huge range of ski designs flood the market, but there is nothing to be gained from having performance skis until you know how to use them. It is only important that the skis you have are the right stiffness and length for your weight. The Madshus website contains all the technical information you could wish for, and they produce skis for all levels of skier, including several of the world's best.

When you put a ski, any ski, onto a flat surface, you will notice that the tip and tail are in contact with that surface, but the middle is slightly arched. This is called the camber of the ski and is critical to the ski's performance. The purpose of the camber is to spread the weight of the skier more evenly over the length of the ski, allowing it to slide more efficiently on snow. Here the similarity between downhill skis and x-country skis ends. Robust Alpine skis are tilted onto one metal edge or the other most of the time because that is how the skier controls speed and direction. X-country skis stay flat in the ruts for all but the most extreme hills. They are designed to be as light as possible, bearing in mind that you will have to propel them forward with every step. Track skis have no metal edges and no heel binding to pamper you on a downhill stretch – Alpine skiers will need to revisit the snowplough and learn to balance over the middle of the ski!

Camber

The camber is actually a double camber. At the risk of being overly technical, I think it might help if you grasped an understanding of why these skis are constructed the way they are. When you stand with your weight distributed evenly over both skis, you effectively flatten out the first camber. The skis will be almost in full contact with the ground, but not quite. The middle section of each will still be a little raised. It is only when you have all your weight over one ski and press down intentionally that it will fully flatten. That is the second camber. Now comes the clever part. You should have your weight spread over both skis when you are going downhill, and sort of gently over one ski for a part of each stride when sliding on the flat. The middle section of the ski base is not being pressed into the snow in either case. So we have what is called a 'glide' wax under both ends of the skis to help them slide better, and a 'kick' wax under the middle section to make the ski grab the snow when we press down on one ski only. The kick wax gives us the friction we wanted under the bars of soap that were mentioned earlier.

You will grasp the concept in five seconds flat when you have a ski in front of you and see how it works. Suffice to say, you press one ski down to make it stick, then launch yourself forward onto the other ski, which will slide forwards for a short distance. That action is repeated in a fluid graceful rhythm to produce the 'diagonal gait' of classic x-country skiing.

An unweighted ski contacts the snow at the tip and the tail.

Even weight over both skis will distribute snow contact along the whole length.

Pressing down on one ski only will allow the middle section of that ski to have increased contact with the snow.

Wax or waxless

Before you become tangled in the mystical world of ski waxes, you might like to know about the other option. These are 'no wax' or 'waxless' skis, similar in design, but instead of wax under the middle part of the ski, there are rows of ribs or fish-scales, all pointing backwards so that they grip the snow when you press down. Waxless skis do not grip as well as properly prepared regular skis, nor do they slide as well. The high friction makes them buzz loudly going downhill. If you can live with the condescending glances from other skiers, and can't be doing with all the fussing about with wax, then by all means give them a try. Actually, to be fair, there are some days in the spring when it is impossible to apply a wax that will work well. You see, each wax has a snow type and temperature range for which it will operate properly, and some days can start well below zero but reach 15 or 20 above by noon. Add altitude differences and shade variations to this and you might well have to re wax several times in one day. You might be forgiven for using waxless in such circumstances.

Waxing area

You can divide a ski into three sections for the purposes of waxing. The middle section, often referred to as the kicking area, needs to be worked out reasonably accurately to ensure that you give the wax every chance to do a good job. Find the point directly under the heel of your boot when attached to the ski. This gives you the rearmost point for any grip wax. Now take the distance from there to a point under the binding assembly, in other words, the length of your boot, and this will give you the halfway point. The whole kick-wax area is therefore a boot length either side of the binding. As a rule, you could say that you always apply kick wax from the heel point, but the amount you go forward will reduce slightly with the more sticky waxes. The rest of the ski base is all glide wax area, and requires little or no attention from a recreational skier. As long as the base has a slightly soapy feel and is reasonably smooth looking, it will do the job perfectly well. The ski shop has a vested interest in applying the glide wax because the base can dry out too much without it. One application should last several weeks.

Kick wax

This is an introduction to waxing, so I apologise to ski technicians and purists in advance for my cavalier attitude to this highly specialised skill.

As I mentioned, you can basically forget about glide wax until you own your own skis. The kick waxes are a different story. One of two things will happen if you have the wrong kick wax on your skis. Either you have too much grip, in which case the snow will bind under the skis and you walk along with a great clump of snow permanently stuck to the wax, or you have too little grip, in which case your skis will slip back a bit when you try to walk forward, so much of the work has to be done with the poles, and believe me, your arms soon become exhausted up any sort of a hill. It is definitely worth the effort to learn the ground rules; apart from making the skis go better, you will be in a position to give your considered opinions and enter heated discussions on the merits of 'klister' over 'red extra' or some such. When I have a beginners group, I will always spend the first half an hour or so in the wax room with them showing how to apply the wax they will need for that day and generally getting them comfortable with the whole concept. Rustad Hotel has a large and convenient wax room, which Erik and Annie allow me to use, even for guests who are not staying at their cosy converted old mountain lodge.

This next section will become more understandable when you peek over someone's shoulder in the hotel wax room, so don't bother grappling with it, just try to get a general feel for now.

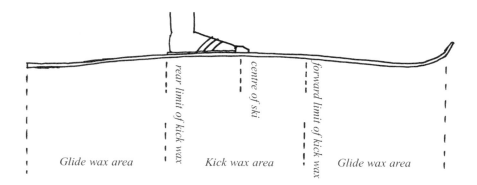

Pot wax

Kick wax is the generic term for all the various concoctions that go under the middle part of the ski. Various makes of wax are available, but the Swix factory is just around the corner, in Lillehammer, and they produce a comprehensive and highly respected range of waxes, poles, clothing and accessories, so I will refer mainly to their products for the sake of simplicity.

Wax that is used at temperatures of 5°c and colder comes in little pots, each of which is colour coded with the appropriate temperature range written on it. The coldest snow requires the hardest wax, consistency of which is similar to candle wax. The basic range goes from greens, the coldest, through blues, violets to reds, which are very tacky and therefore tricky to apply evenly. Every few years, Swix tweak their formulas a bit, design some new artwork for their pots and produce a new range. Some serious skiers spend a fortune on waxes for a marginal improvement in performance. Ski preparation is one of those activities that will always fill the time available, and Swix produce lots of interesting looking gadgets, very few of which will you need initially. If you are smart enough to go skiing when the snow is cold, you will have the bonus of very easy and effective waxing. Wait until spring and suffer the consequences!

So there you are standing in the wax room of the hotel armed with the brand new tin of 'blue extra' as recommended by a fellow guest (of many years experience), who's advice was punctured by supporting comments from other guests. Having given you the collective benefit of their many years of experience, you find yourself deserted and left to figure out how to proceed.

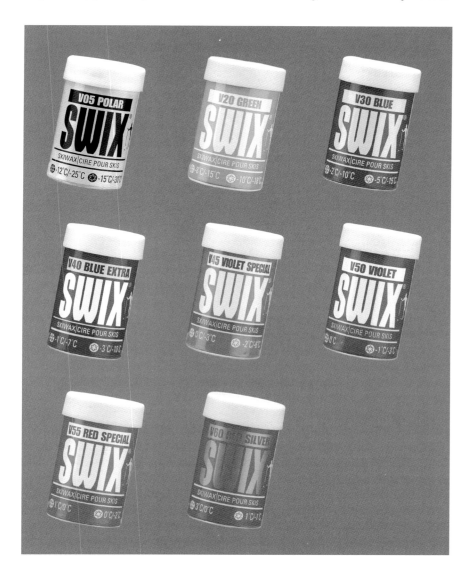

Application of wax

Take the top off the pot and peel about .5cm of the metal foil all the way round. Use a fingernail to start it going. When you replace the top, any exposed wax will be covered if you don't remove too much foil. Now rub a thin layer of wax all over the kick area, ignoring the groove. This wax goes on just like candle wax, so hold the pot vertically and rub along the ski in firm strokes. A thin layer is enough, and you are now going to spread it out anyway, so there is no need to be neat. At this point you are about to find out why the chap in the shop made you buy a block of cork or a synthetic equivalent. Use the cork flat, and vigorously rub a small area at a time to heat the wax to make it spread and sink into the ski a bit. When the wax starts to disappear, then you have won. Personally, I do this operation once only, but in the official Swix manual, they recommend four or five layers. Undoubtedly the wax will last better, but I can't help thinking of the toothpaste advert where the entire length of the toothbrush is piled high with paste – does anybody really do that? There is an easier way to spread kick wax, and some hotels cater for this. You can use a heated iron to melt the wax into the ski. Keep the iron moving all the time or you could blister the base material. An iron is great to have for the softer waxes, because one tends to get lumps all over the place, and they are hard to spread out with a cork.

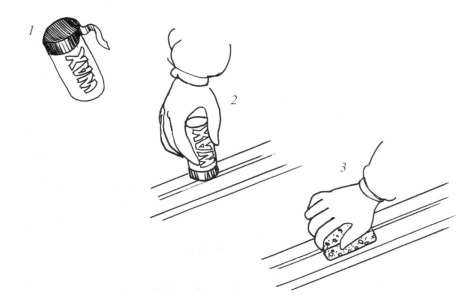

Waxing outside

Before you put your skis on, you will need to let them stand outside for a while to cool down to the working temperature of the wax. If you did start skiing straight away, it might take a few minutes before you feel any grip under the skis. Cold waxes, the greens and blues, tend to last much better than the warm ones. Snow, particularly old snow, acts like sandpaper and will remove wax after a few kilometres. This is why we carry a couple of waxes with us; partly because we might need to re-wax, but also we might need to change waxes. If conditions stay consistent throughout the day, it is just a question of picking up a ski, holding the front end with one hand while the heel is wedged against your foot, and rubbing in a new layer of the same wax. There really is no need to be thorough about this, a fast vigorous rub to cover the kick area, followed by a once over with the heel of your bare hand is adequate.

The later in the season it is, the more likely it is to warm up during the day. The blue you put on first thing has stopped working after only a couple of hours, and when you inspect your skis, you see that there is plenty of wax still there. You will need to apply a layer of a warmer wax over the existing blue. When changing from a colder to a warmer wax, you can simply rub it straight on, because the warmer the wax, the stickier it is, so it can be spread without disturbing the layer underneath. Even using a cork will work fine. Once in a while, you might need to reduce the amount of grip you are getting. Rub in a colder wax than the one you have on to create a cocktail of the two.

In effect, you are 'blinding' the stickier wax. Too much grip means that the snow cannot be scraped off easily, thereby preventing any sliding. This is the plodding along on platform shoes look – even snowshoes would be preferable. Poor technique makes this problem far more likely to occur, but waxing is definitely a major factor. By the end of the day, your various experiments with wax may have led to an interesting looking stodge under the skis. A thorough clean up might be in order, but before we go into that, we should discuss the nightmare known as klister.

Klister

This is a viscous wax with attitude. It is sold in tubes like tooth paste, it is extremely tacky and gets everywhere. Don't be surprised if it turns up on your kitchen tap in middle of summer. A full temperature range of klisters is available, though why anyone would want to use klister instead of a pot wax whenever possible is a mystery. Having said that, klisters do last much better when the tracks are icy, and if you are in a competition, the last thing you need is to have to stop and rewax. There comes a point on warm spring days when even the red pot wax will not grip. Up to about 3°c one can get away with pot waxes, but beyond that point klister takes over, because it is able to deal with the higher levels of free water within the snow. Tube klisters take a bit of getting used to, but there is a user-friendly product called universal klister, which has a wide temperature range, enabling newcomers to have a reasonable chance to get their skis running properly. You can buy it in tube form, but I suggest that you go for the aerosol can. An aerosol can labelled 'quick kick' is the universal klister for colder temperatures, and is a good solution for icy tracks. When you remove the top of one of these aerosols you will see a spongy pad, through which the klister is forced when you press straight down onto the ski. Just dab blotches along the kick zone, maybe eight or nine, then gently spread the almost liquid goo along the kick zone in a very few, slow strokes. You will now have a permanently sticky, shiny layer of treacherous gunk just waiting to get stuck to hair, gloves, clothes and everything else. Take the can with you in its own plastic bag, making sure that it does not come in direct contact with anything. If you get some on your hands, when out and about, a rub with orange peel will reduce the stickiness.

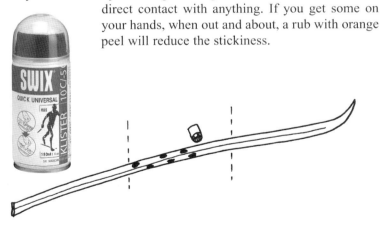

Press the sponge applicator onto the ski and wax will be released through it. Use about eight or nine dabs and gently spread the wax with the sponge.

We can leave the use and application of tube klisters for when you become a bit more familiar with the basics. A colleague of mine used to impress his groups by going outside, sniffing the air, sifting the snow through his fingers and generally looking at one with the mountains before giving his verdict on which combination of klisters would be appropriate for the day. A quick peek at the temperature gauge on the wall outside and a weather printout from the net in his pocket probably helped.

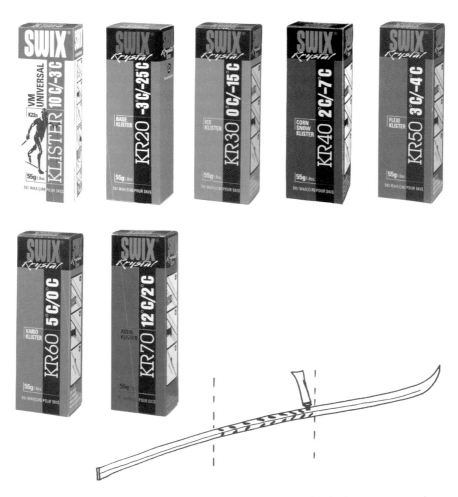

Lay thin chevrons of wax onto the ski, then slowly draw a scraper along to create a solid shiny layer. No rubbing in, drying time or anything else.

Warm snow?

I have been talking about waxes for snow temperatures above zero. That has to be nonsense, of course, because it would be water by definition. Snow can be colder than zero, but not warmer. We are referring to snow temperature and type when selecting waxes below zero. We are referring to air temperature when above zero. The air temperature will indicate how close to melting the snow is; in other words, how much free water is present in the degenerating snow crystals. Water repellent klisters have been developed for wet snow. The factors governing friction vary for different snow types, hence the need for highly specialised waxes to maintain the exact amount of grip we need.

Wax on a strip

This is a roll of pre-waxed tape and is a recent development that is expensive but does take hassle and some decision making out of waxing. It might become the future, but as yet, conventional waxing seems to work better. You simply lay out a strip of tape along the base, either side of the central groove, and either iron it on or just press it down, depending on which brand you have. A wide temperature range means that it will function all day, and one set is robust enough to last several days. Serious skiers don't seem to have taken to it yet, they liken the strip's performance to waxless skis, but it is still early days.

Apply like double-sided tape.

Cleaning skis

You really only need to clean your skis when an existing wax is softer than the one you wish to apply, or if you have a load of debris stuck to the underside of your skis. The former can happen quite often in spring, for when you step outside first thing in the morning, it will feel a bit parky compared to the tee shirt skiing of the previous afternoon. Again, in the spring, or after strong winds, all sorts of bits of tree and fibres can find their way into the ruts. Klister will pick up every scrap more efficiently than a vacuum cleaner.

For cleaning the skis, you will need a scraper, some loo paper or similar and a can of base cleaner. Swix sell a hand cleaner in a tube. A tiny amount of this stuff does a much better job than any amount of soap. Sticky hands are guaranteed when cleaning skis.

First you should try to find some way of securing the ski with the base uppermost. There will probably be a vice you can use in the wax room. Scrape the worst off first by holding the scraper at an angle, as though you were removing flaky paint, and wipe it after every stroke on a piece of paper soaked in base cleaner. Press quite hard and try to get a bow wave of wax rucking up against the leading edge of your scraper. You won't get it all off, only the worst. Now wet the whole area liberally with base cleaner, even taking in the sides of the ski. Leave the solvent to work for half a minute before having another go with the scraper, and any residue wax will be dissolved by a rub with your soaked cloth. Follow that with a final wipe down using a dry one. If you are re-waxing immediately, a slightly greasy ski means a film of cleaner still persists, and can stop new wax from adhering for a moment. You just have to keep rubbing. There is nothing clever here, except perhaps the art of goo control, but ski preparation is definitely relevant to your enjoyment of this sport.

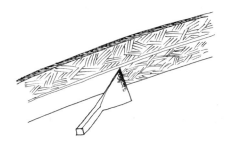

Chapter 3

Practical section

Fitness

X-country skiing is one of very few sports that are perfectly suited to the natural movements of the body. You don't have the twisting or jerking of many, you don't have the overuse of some muscle groups, often at the expense of others, and you don't have any unusual or awkward body positions to assume. It has taken evolution many thousands of years to develop forward motion on two legs in a balanced, rhythmic action. X-country uses and actually improves this skill. You will learn to co-ordinate every muscle group in your body to produce a smooth, relaxed and therapeutic set of movements. A few days of skiing will inevitably improve your general health, and will often alleviate injuries, both new and long term. As your technique improves, your confidence will grow and you will be able to relax more. You become more economic, allowing the body's natural rhythm and timing to take over.

The equipment is light and comfortable and you choose how hard and fast you work. By taking things at your own speed, you need only try things that you feel ready for. It does the confidence no good to fall on a hill that you did not like the look of anyway. Just take off your skis and walk down the worst of it. Serious injuries are extremely rare, a bruised backside and damaged pride are normally as bad as it gets.

People who keep themselves in reasonable shape will find no difficulty taking on the unfamiliar techniques, it helps to have the habit of taking some regular exercise and doing a bit of general stretching, but frankly anyone who is prepared to have a go, will get a lot out of it.

If you want to do a bit of pre-season training, there are two areas of the body that can become sore when skiing; one is the triceps, the other is the groin. Triceps (the muscles under your upper arms) can suffer because the action of pulling yourself along with a pair of overgrown walking sticks is not something we do every day. The groin area can be overworked if you try to go too fast or your technique is poor. Always travel at a speed that allows you to carry on a normal conversation with a fellow skier. That way you won't use up your energy reserves too quickly and you won't overwork your groin muscles. Even though the skis and boots are very light, you have added some weight to each foot. Over a few thousand steps, the extra weight can cause strain if you overdo it. Good technique makes a big difference.

The secret of enjoying a day out is to take it at a gentle pace and savour the peace and quiet. One can ski for an entire day without seeing another soul – that is an interesting experience in itself. Sometimes the only sound is your own heartbeat, and nothing is moving for as far as the eye can see. If it weren't for the tracks and patches of cleared woodland on distant hills, there would be no sign of human presence. To some that is a real tonic and to others it is a bit intimidating.

Painful groin?
Spread your knees until it hurts, then hold
for 10 seconds! Do this a couple of times
before and after skiing.

Ski lessons

I used to thoroughly enjoy ski school when I was learning alpine skiing. It was four hours per day for six days. The instructor was as much a shepherd as a teacher. He would lead us to the head of lift queues and find excellent watering holes. We picked up some technique as we went along, but ski school was not just about drills and exercises, it was the company, the laughs and the structured fun that a good instructor can provide. It is possible to enjoy a similar atmosphere with x-country, especially if you come as part of a group. That way, you will have readymade company, and lessons and guides become cheaper per head. Ole Berg runs an impressive venue, for both small and large groups, based at his traditional Norwegian farm about 15 mins. south of Lillehammer. He won official recognition at the Olympics as the venue with outstanding quality and atmosphere. The top brass of Coca Cola, the official sponsors, held their own main event there. The list of possibilities for activities is only limited by the size of your budget! Groups will often bring their own guides with them, but it can be potluck as to how much help you will get with technique. People who book independently will usually have to take private lessons as there are rarely enough beginners to warrant group type ski school.

The good news is that a beginner of average ability only needs four hours instruction in total. Two hours on their first morning, ideally, and two hours on, say, the third day. In those four hours, you should receive enough information to keep you busy for the week.

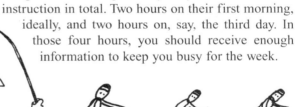

An ambitious student might well benefit from a further session to refine and develop their basic technique. Nervous newcomers often take a bit longer to get their confidence, and might well benefit from a gentler learning curve. It is often possible to hire an instructor as a guide for the day, but be prepared for a different sort of a day!

Nedre Berg Gård

Arrangements for groups from 10-200 people in and around the Lillehammer Olympic area.

- Corporate entertainment
- Team building
- Group activities

A selection of activities:
- Ice driving tuition (left hand drive)
- Snow scooters around a private circuit
- Piloted bobsleigh down the olympic run
- Horse riding on Islandic horses
- Helicopter rides over mountains and glaciers
- Mushing your own dog team
- Alpine, Telemark and cross-country skiing whit tuition

A selection of entertainments:
- Various museums and exhibitions
- An eventing meal in a Lapp tent with entertainment
- Medieval dinner, Viking style
- Private pub with entertainment
- Watch an ice hockey match/ski jumping/ski racing

Nedre Berg Gård,
2372 Brøttum
tel: +47 62 36 01 08
mobile:+47 908 98 425
oleb2@online.no
www.oleberg.no

Learning to ski

It is time to put the skis on and have a go. This section explains what to do in a step-by-step format. You don't have to perform each exercise perfectly before progressing, but you do need to feel that you have understood what is wanted and can make a passable attempt at each drill. Repetition is the key to success. Do something several times and the feedback from each new attempt will give the muscles more and more information. Eventually, experience lets you know what to expect and muscle memory enables you to handle it. So 'practice' is really repetition of an activity to promote familiarity. This in turn generates confidence, which allows you to concentrate without being distracted by fear. If you choose to be your own teacher, you would do well to follow the system laid out over the next few pages and be a bit tough on yourself. You will learn more quickly and prevent bad habits if you pay close attention to the basics. Sorry to sound so heavy, but the above is fundamental to learning and even qualified teachers can get it wrong. Spending too long on a drill is as unprofessional as not long enough.

Practice makes perfect, but when it becomes boring, you can do it well enough, so move on!

One ski

Find a quiet area of track at least 50m long and dead flat. Now lie one ski on firm snow, and set the other one to one side. We only need one ski and two poles for the moment. You will notice that there is a bar on the front of the boot. This fits neatly into a groove behind the rubbery bit on the binding. If you have a sprung system, the bar will simply click into place. If you have a lever system, you will need to open the lever first, then place your foot on the binding with the bar in the groove, and close the lever. Either way, make sure that there is no snow trapped between your boot and the bar. If you get ice in the workings, it can be a devil of a job to sort things out. An easy way to clear the bar is to pick up your foot and tap the bar with the metal shaft of your pole until the snow falls off. Now align your boot exactly straight and centrally on the binding and press straight down. Well-used boots will often be quite bowed, so you might have to lift your heel to get the bar to engage. To release the ski, press and hold down the plastic panel on the front of the binding, using either your other foot or the point of your pole, and simply step off. With a lever system, you will have to bend down and open the lever to release.

Put the ski on again and grab a pole in each hand. Don't bother with the straps for now, just use the poles for balance. Remembering to drive on the right, put your ski in one of the ruts such that you will not destroy the other rut with your free foot.

The author's guestroom. Photo: Keith Richardson

Stick-scrape

Just walk as normally as possible, using small steps, and pressing straight down on the ski every time it stops. That press makes the kick wax do it's job, and the ski should feel rooted to the snow for a moment. You won't be able to do this if your weight is not directly over the front ski. This is the single most important skill you need to acquire. When walking without skis on, we place the heel down first. The body pivots over that foot and continues forward. We bring the other foot through in time to prevent ourselves falling forward. When skiing, the whole foot is slid forward with all our weight going with it, not after it. Thus, we have to balance over the front foot while it is moving. The purpose of this exercise is to show that the same ski can be asked to slide or stop dead, depending on what we do with our weight and pressure. If you pick the ski up even a bit while it is on it's forward journey, two things can go wrong. Firstly, your groin muscles will eventually complain about lugging the extra weight, and secondly, the snow that sticks to the ski when you press it will not be scraped off between presses. A lump of snow under your ski would prevent it from gliding. 'Glide' is the slide moment between each step when you ride the front ski until it runs out of momentum.

Gliding on one ski

When you have been up and down your bit of track a few times practicing step-scrape, step-scrape, it is time to try to get the ski to glide. The knack here is to launch yourself onto the front ski smoothly enough not to trigger the kick wax. Use your other foot and both poles to propel yourself along, trying to stand on the ski as much as possible and definitely never lifting it. Don't expect a smooth ride, this is hard enough to do without wax under the ski, but persevere until you have felt the sensation of standing on a ski that is moving. If your wax is too aggressive, it is extremely difficult to get any glide, and you will probably become disheartened and believe that you are at fault. Just rub a slightly colder wax over what you have to 'blind' it a bit, and see if that goes better. Most skis can be used on either foot, as there is usually no left and right. Start with the first exercise again, alternating feet once in a while, and taking plenty of breaks.

Weight transfer

If you are worried about putting the other ski on, then you need to do more practice on one ski. You should always feel ready for each new phase. When you do put them both on, you will have some friction between the wax and the snow, giving you the impression that the skis are stable. Even a small adjustment of your weight can cause a ski to slip unexpectedly, so don't trust them an inch. Move carefully, with small steps, and go for a slow walk in the ruts doing the press – scrape, press – scrape as you go. Use your poles for balance all the time. The body has to move side to side, from one ski to the other, in order to be able to apply a good press through the middle of the ski. This is another aspect of skiing that does not come automatically, for when we walk without skis, we place the feet close enough to a straight line that the weight transfer is negligible. By rolling the body slightly, you shift your weight over each ski. Now we need to find the exact centre of each ski. As you walk along, look down at your boots; if you can see more than just your toes, then your weight is back of middle or your legs are too straight or both. A long stride makes it hard to get onto the front ski, so for now, use small steps and think about walking with the knee hiding most of your foot. This will bring your whole body forward onto the front ski earlier than before, and that is what we are after. Now when you press the ski at the exact moment it stops, you will be pressing straight down through the middle of the ski, creating a moment of grip that will allow you to launch yourself forward onto the other ski.

Try walking quickly for a few steps and giving a push with both poles at once, if your weight is even over both skis, they should glide quite well, depending on conditions. Becoming familiar with how to make a ski glide is as important as how to make it stick.

Sinking in

The untracked snow beside you is often possible to walk in without sinking down more than a few inches. Here is a useful exercise; try walking in a straight line with your feet apart as though you were still in the ruts and press hard enough to make the skis sink in at least a bit. As you walk, rolling the body and pressing each foot in rhythm, have a look at your skis. If they tilt sideways as they sink into the loose snow when you press, then you are not standing directly over that ski. It takes quite a while to develop the knack of perfect weight transfer, but it improves automatically and eventually feels quite natural if you persist. Another benefit of loose snow is that you have a chance to test how straight you can keep your feet. Look back at your tracks after you have gone 50m and check whether you have two perfect tramlines or should you be breathalysed?

Pacing yourself

You are bound to see skiers of all standards, with all sorts of styles. Perhaps the commonest fault is that the poles are not being used efficiently. This is understandable because very few people have strong triceps, so they tire quickly and have to resort to leg power for propulsion. Ideally, a skier should generate up to 30% of their momentum from the arms alone, but to do that over any distance would require many hours of training. It is not uncommon for a top athlete to snap a pole through sheer force; next time you are watching a race, look for coaches and trainers dotted around, carrying spare poles! A recreational skier can reasonably expect to muster about 10% of their momentum from poles initially, and to overdo it will just make your muscles sore.

A sound understanding of technique and good balance will prevent a host of unnecessary aches and pains. If you are with a group who travel at too fast a pace for you, then you will learn very little, struggle all the time and almost certainly begin to regret the whole idea. Much better to go at your own pace, by yourself if necessary, and meet up later. Handing in your skis in exchange for snowshoes is the skiing equivalent of taking to drink. For some it is all about distance covered, for others it is how they do it, but for most of us, it is enough to be on skis, on holiday and on a gentle learning curve.

Using poles

Sooner or later you are going to come
to a hill. I would recommend a policy
of removing your skis and walking up
or down anything you don't like the
look of. Find a gentle up hill, just steep
enough that your skis want to slide back all the
time. This is where we start to use the poles for
more than just balancing. Assuming that the
strap at the top is a simple loop, there is no
difference between left and right. Wiggle your
whole gloved hand up through the loop from
below, then grab the strap and handle, together, in
your fist. Hold the handle loosely and pull down

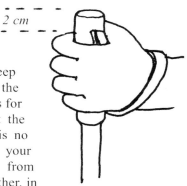

2 cm

against the strap. If the strap is correctly adjusted, the handle will protrude
about 2cm above your closed hand, while pulling down against the
supporting strap. From the first moment you start to wear straps, try to
loosen your grip on the poles and rely on the straps as much as possible. One
reason for this is that a tight grip will restrict blood circulation through your
fingers, making them unnecessarily cold and tired; and another is that you
will eventually learn to actually let go of your poles as part of each stride,
when you become a bit more accomplished.

Up hill

The length of your poles is becoming relevant now. If you try to propel
yourself forward by using only your poles, you will naturally raise your
arms to about chest height in front of you, bending them slightly, and plant
the poles into the snow at a considerable angle, pointing backwards to get
the leverage. This angle is important, because on the up hills you get
holding power against sliding backwards, and on the flat you get forward
momentum. When you first start to use poles, they are really only out-
riggers to help with balance. You have to raise your arms quite high to
plant the poles wide apart, forward of your feet. As you gain more
confidence, you will be able to bring your arms in and down, such that the
poles will be planted behind the feet while the arms are lifted forward only
to a comfortable height. Alpine skiers often have difficulty losing their old
habits, they will insist on planting their poles vertically, which means that

every stride, their shoulders have to hoist all that extra weight of arm. The trick is to swing your arms naturally when you are walking on skis, almost dragging your poles. Just let the pole enter the snow wherever it happens to be, probably quite close in and a little behind your foot. Now the pole will be steeply angled, and you can pull down on the strap immediately.

Exactly that system will allow you to climb even severe hills straight up, depending on how much grip you have under the skis and how strong your arms are. Take shorter steps and make an exaggerated press of each ski to maximise grip; you are even allowed to lift your feet slightly to help with the press, but don't tell anyone I said so. Lean heavily on each strap in turn to help prevent the skis from suddenly losing grip and shooting back, causing you to fall forward onto your knees.

On the flat

The more you ski, the more you will realise that good technique is all about being economic with your movements, but effective at the same time. Learning to co-ordinate the poles and the skis is fundamental. When you are walking with no glide, the stride pattern is small and rapid. If the arms are to stay in rhythm with the legs, then they must only travel a small distance as well. Let the arms swing freely from the shoulders, exactly as though you were walking with nothing in your hands. Your hands should swing in an arc in time with your legs. The size of the arc will need to get bigger if you start to stride out, otherwise you will lose synchronisation. If you watch someone running on skis with a lengthy glide between each powerful thrust of the legs, then there is a surprisingly long moment between pole plants. Either the skier must move their arms very slowly to prevent losing timing, or they must use a much bigger arm swing to still be able to thrust with the poles. The skier will reach forward and up as far as a right angle, extending each arm fully behind them with pressure on the strap the whole way. Very impressive to see how fast they can go over enormous distances. There is an annual race held here each spring. 11,000 skiers travel 58km over three mountains, and the leaders take about 2.5hrs. It commemorates the route taken by two soldiers some 800yrs ago, when they were escorting the boy king to safety. It took them three days, and they did well to survive.

Pole action

A good pole action has the hands held low, the arms kept almost straight the whole time and the appropriate size of arc with the hand being extended behind the body every stride. This applies to any speed of skiing. One nicety that allows the fingers to move all the time, and therefore keep warm, is to partially or completely release the handle of the pole at the last moment, and, still pulling down on the strap, give a tweak with the wrist to produce a little extra thrust. The pole can be gathered between the forefinger and thumb on the way forward, and fully gripped in time for the next plant. Watch any good skier and you will see how this is done.

Half herringbone

Some hills are too severe to climb straight up. The skis will slip back no matter how well you use the poles. Without breaking stride or changing rhythm, pick up the left ski and place it outside the rut at an angle of about 45°. (We use the left one because the edge of the track is on our right, where the snow can be difficult.) If you tilt your foot slightly, the edge of your ski will bite into the snow, and you can walk up trusting the angled ski and your poles. It does not matter if the skis cross at the back, because your right ski is still in the rut and therefore below your left one, so they will never actually touch. It is possible to walk almost normally, sliding one ski and lifting the other. Use the poles in exactly the same way as usual. Experience will tell you how wide an angle you should have with your left ski, you want just enough to prevent back-slip without wasting energy.

Full herringbone

You have come across a steep hill with no ruts. Other skiers may have smoothed them out when skiing down or maybe wind has obliterated them. You have four reasonable options; go another way, take your skis off and walk up, use diagonal sidestep or use a full herringbone. It might well be worth going up just for the view or whatever, but bear in mind what goes up must come down. The diagonal sidestep is as it sounds, and we shall look at that soon, but the herringbone needs some explanation.

It is called herringbone because of the pattern the skis make in the snow. The skis are held in a V shape, so your feet have to be well apart. When walking forward, each ski has to be lifted slightly off the snow and replaced still in the V formation. Your weight has to shift side to side with every step and both skis need to be slightly on their edges all the time, leaving thin lines behind you in the snow. If a ski slips sideways while doing this, you are not edging your ski enough or you are not transferring enough weight over to it. If it slips backwards, then either you need to widen the V, or use the poles more aggressively.

Here is a painless way to get the feel of this technique. Start in the middle of the flat part of the track, and walk with small steps, lifting each ski slightly and tramping it down again. Holding your poles wide apart, bang them home in time with your feet. When your right foot clomps down, your left pole should hit the snow beside your left foot, and vice versa. Get this rhythm going, with your skis flat and pointing forwards. When you start up the hill, let the ski tips separate and start to shift your weight side to side. The skis will cross at the back if you do not spread your feet enough, but when you look behind you, you will see that by placing each foot up and out just the right amount, the skis will interlock without interfering with each other. If they do touch at the back, then the edge of the ski on top will not grip and will slide away. As it gets steeper, lean forward a bit and tilt your skis onto their inside edges more to get extra bite. Rely on your poles rather than your skis and make you way up in a plodding zigzag, committing all your weight to one ski then the other. Once you get the hang of this, it will work well for every snow type except sheet ice and deep snow, both of which you should try to avoid at this stage.

Fall line

'Fall line' is the route a ball would take when rolling down a hill. The fall line on the exact piece of snow you are standing on can be quite different from the general fall line of the hill. When your skis are 'across the fall line' they are not pointing up or down hill, but are completely level. A track that winds around a hill will often have a significant tilt to it. It can be frustrating to have your skis refusing to stay put, so try this: work out the fall line for the bit of snow you are standing on, and draw a line with your pole where you think it runs. Now place your skis across that line at 90°, and tilt the skis onto their top edges to bite into the snow. Your skis have to behave.

Diagonal sidestep

Occasionally you will come across a section of track that is tilted as well as up hill. If you ski along the track and try using a herringbone, the lower ski will be pointing across the hill and will grip very easily on its edge, but the other ski will be pointing straight up the fall line. The herringbone is most effective when the skis are placed equally either side of the fall line. A useful technique here is the diagonal sidestep.

Place your skis across the fall line and slightly on their top edges. You will now be able to walk forward, keeping the skis on the snow all the time. If your tilted track goes gently up hill, you can still walk normally, following the hill, using your poles properly and keeping just enough edge on your skis to prevent them from slipping sideways. A steeper hill will become too much for your arms, so change the angle of your ascent by allowing your ski tips to drop down closer to 'across the fall line' and you can relax immediately. In order to gain height while moving forward, lift the top ski and place it out sideways, up the hill a comfortable amount. You will need to pay special attention to keeping that ski parallel to the lower one, because what tends to happen is that your foot turns out, so the tip gets turned up the hill, and suddenly you are slipping back, the skis cross at the back and it all goes pear-shaped. The secret is to intentionally make an effort to get the tail of the ski away from you. You will feel that your foot is a bit turned in, as though you are walking pigeon-toed. When you bring the other foot up to join the top one, thereby closing the skis again, it will move easily and you can take it forward a good way. The poles should both be planted simultaneously with the top ski. By planting them vertically, they are used mainly for balance and for hoisting your weight up onto the top ski every step. Thus you are progressing up and forwards at the same time, leaving a series of parallel lines in pairs behind you in the snow.

Occasionally conditions are such that you can leave the tracks and strike out over virgin terrain. You can climb very successfully using diagonal sidestep in a series of long traverses. Move in a steady rhythm, changing direction regularly to rest the lead leg.

Down hill

Skiing down a hill can be everything from exhilarating to very frightening. To start with you need to find a slope that is steep enough to allow the skis to run evenly for a few seconds before flattening out. You do not have brakes yet, so for the time being, it would be kind to your backside if you walked down anything that looked like it required speed control. Using the bottom section of a long slope is not advisable because some skiers seem to have a death wish, and you are likely to be in their way.

Prepare a good downhill body position on a flat area. Stand with your weight spread over both feet evenly, with everything bent a bit, much like a goalkeeper facing a penalty, the only difference being that your feet will be closer together. The position is the same as for alpine skiing, except that there is no boot to press the shin against. That can throw old time alpine skiers until they learn to weight their whole foot, rather than the front half. Modern carving skis require the weight to be more central, which makes these two forms of skiing mutually beneficial.

Always start a downhill run by walking forward, sliding the skis hard to clear them of any lumps stuck to the kick wax. When they are gliding freely, assume the goalkeeper position and do nothing. Just go for the ride and try to feel through your feet. The skis will travel very smoothly, so if you lose your balance, it is nearly always a question of confidence. Try bending everything a bit more, to lower your centre of gravity, and try again, this time with a little more faith. When your skis begin to slow down, start to walk just before you would come to a stop. At very slow speeds, the wax can start to grip again, so by walking you will prevent sudden jerks. If you take on bigger hills and find yourself out of control, the lesser of various evils is to sit straight down on your skis. This is quite hard to do elegantly, but possible. Avoid colliding with trees at all costs, pine trees are not so bad, but spruce and fir tend to lose their lower branches, leaving short spears sticking straight out.

Getting up

Gravity will occasionally get the better of you, and you find yourself in an undignified heap. If you are on the flat, just hoist your skis around until they are side by side and you are sitting beside them. If you are on a slope, same thing, but you need to sit on the uphill side of the skis having got your skis across the fall line. Keep your poles on, but don't use them yet. Leaving your skis exactly where they are, raise yourself onto your hands and knees and work your way around in a big circle until your knees are on top of your skis. Now slide one ski forward so that you are kneeling on one ski only, and by planting a pole each side, pull yourself up. The secret is not to struggle; if you jerk yourself around at awkward angles, you can easily pull muscles or worse. There is usually a logical way to untangle yourself if you take a moment to work it out. Sometimes an ankle complains when doing the crab imitation on hands and knees. This will be because your nearer foot is lying sideways on the snow while your knees are working their way around to the front. The pain will magically disappear if you simply tilt that ski so that it lies flat instead of on it's side. That gets the ankle off the snow and in line with the rest of your leg.

A fall in deep snow can prove an exhausting experience. The technique for getting up is the same, but you might need to take off your poles to use them as a platform to prevent your arms from sinking in while you manoeuvre. If things don't work out, you can always take off one or both skis by carefully aiming the tip of a pole at the release mechanism and jabbing hard. This can still be done from a variety of interesting positions.

This chap's left ankle will be agonising in (a) until he lifts it as in (b).

Balance

Some people have more natural balance than others, that is true, but when you consider the extraordinary feat of learning to walk in the first place, you can see that the balance required for skiing is only a minor extension of that same ability. Small children are notoriously fearless and therefore learn very effectively simply by imitation. The older one is, the more knocks one has filed away in the 'to be avoided' folder, and a red light appears when situations arise which might add to that folder. This makes one less confident, less relaxed and less focused on new activities. Also, adults have a much harder time learning muscle co-ordination for new movements. You can often recognise a late starter in tennis or golf, for example, by their unique interpretation of the textbook. If you can turn off the red light and trust your body to do what it does naturally, x-country skiing becomes a walk in the park. Now and again a customer will have a confidence problem, and every time they begin to slide, they immediately sit down. This can become a vicious circle; they will not stay up until they know what will happen, but they can't find out what will happen until they stay up! It helps to try to trust your body and to concentrate on feeling for balance through the feet, but it is still you who has to do it. I tried to help one lady who was terrified to try anything because she was physically unable to raise herself from her knees to her feet. Understandably, the mere thought of falling completely removed any willingness to learn technique. She was much happier walking the tracks on foot. You don't have to be in the least sporty to enjoy x-country skiing, but it does help to be in reasonable physical condition.

Starting on a hill

There will be times when you are
standing with your skis across the fall line
and you want to get into the ruts and slide
down. An experienced skier doesn't
bother with the following manoeuvre,
but it is nice to do things slowly for the
first few times. Check uphill to make
sure the track is clear, and then walk
over until you are standing over the
ruts, remembering to keep your skis
on their edges all the time. Plant one
pole each side of the ruts and far
enough down so that you are
actually leaning on them when
your arms and poles are in a
straight line. You will need to
almost let go of the poles and
rely on the straps for this, or put
your hands on top of the poles. If you
have done this properly, it is effortless to hold
yourself back while you turn your skis
through 90° with several little steps, and you
will have plenty of room. If you don't plant
your poles far enough away, you might well
slide forward when trying to turn your skis,
then the poles get in the way and disaster
looms. When you are ready, start by
walking with a good hard scrape to get
the skis running well and just ski
down with your skis side by side in
the goalkeeper position. When
sliding at any speed at all, the hands
should be in front of the body with
the poles pointing back. This is
automatic with a good basic body
position.

Changing tracks

The challenge here is to somehow lift the skis out of one set of ruts and put them back either in the same ruts or another set, while on the move. This is a useful option to have when there is an obstacle in your way. A short series of exercises can make this easier to learn.

Find a gentle hill in a quiet spot, one with well defined ruts.1) Start by doing a couple of runs down to get the feel of the speed and the snow; 2) try bending down and touching your toes several times, always feeling for balance through your feet; 3) slowly shift your weight onto one ski and lift the tip of the other just off the snow for a moment. Do this a few times alternating the feet slowly and gently on the way down to improve your balance.

4) While standing still in the ruts, lift the left ski just enough to get it out of the rut, and place it just outside the rut but still parallel to the right ski. Put all your weight onto it for a moment before replacing it into the rut once more. You will notice that your weight has to transfer three times to do this.

5) Make a few runs trying this on the move, until you can step in and out of the tracks with either foot, in an unhurried, smooth series of actions. Imagine you are skiing on eggs, try to place skis softly and move weight smoothly; jerky actions can cause the wax to grip suddenly or the skis to react strangely.

6) This final phase will be a doddle if you have ever skated or roller-skated. The action is identical, you in effect skate your left foot out of the rut and bring the right foot to it. For the rest of us, we are stepping out as before, but instead of placing the ski parallel, point the tip away a bit. By the time the skis have started to diverge, you should have launched all your weight onto the leading ski, making it possible for the other ski to be pulled out of the rut to join it. That should be done as one continuous flowing movement with no pauses, because if you hesitate with one ski in and one out, you will wind up doing the splits. Think of it as a one-two, with loads of commitment. Now you are out of the ruts and heading down the centre of the track.

You will learn to steer the skis in the next section, but for now we shall find out how to get back into the ruts. This is much easier than it looks. Most people just sort of wobble their way in, having approached the ruts at a very narrow angle. About the only thing that can go wrong is that both skis end up in the same rut. You can avoid that by waiting until your skis are almost falling into the ruts by themselves, and at the last moment, lift the outer ski and reach across to the far rut with it. Your other ski will fall into the nearside rut by itself.

Braking

X-country skis are not designed to turn or brake as their primary function. Heavier, wider skis with metal edges are available, but they are normally used with a heavier boot and are designed for touring away from the tracks, in the 'back country'. I mention this to appease Alpine skiers.

There are a variety of techniques for cornering and slowing down, but with these light track skis, one should think in terms of speed control rather than braking. After only a few days on skis, you will learn to judge how much to check your speed on any given hill. When you can see the track in front flattens out, you can afford to be out of control for a while, because you know you will slow down soon enough. Trying to brake is hard work, and there is no point in wasting energy. Just let your skis have their way, taking care to read ahead as best you can.

One ski snowplough

This is a speed control technique, and as the name infers, you learn to push the snow in front of one ski to create a braking effect. You need to be pretty comfortable with moving your weight from one ski to the other and lifting a ski out of the ruts before you try this exercise. If you can change tracks, then you are more than ready.

A short hill where the snow next to the ruts is reasonably smooth is ideal. Stand in the ruts on a flat section first so that you can feel for the correct body position before you start. The right leg stays put the whole time, but lift the left one out sideways and place it in the snow in a lopsided 'v' with the other ski. The tips should be about 5cm apart, and the heels wide apart. The left foot will be turned in, while the right one remains straight. Lower your centre of gravity by crouching a bit more than usual, and keep your hands both in front of you and wide apart to help with balance. Let the right ski stay flat in the rut, but tilt the left one onto it's inside edge. If your ploughing ski was kept flat when moving downhill, it would catch any ridges or lumps and your skis would cross at the front. Experiment with adjusting the amount of edge you create by rotating your ankle out and back. If you have supple joints or weak ankles, you will need to be particularly careful that the outside edge of your ploughing ski does not catch the snow. Standing in that 'v' position, try to separate the skis a little more by pressing out sideways. Do that a couple of times to learn which muscles you will have to use to keep the 'v' shape when the skis are moving. Now that your feet are further apart, you will have a wide platform to balance on, and remember the goalkeeper with that poised-for-action look.

When you try this out, for the first couple of times, keep nearly all your weight on the right foot and just brush over the snow with the left while in the 'v' position. Gradually add more weight to the left, working to hold the ski steady and slightly on it's edge. Don't let your body twist or tilt; all the work should be done from the waist down, with the body relaxed and remaining central over the skis. The more you press the left ski into the snow, the more friction you generate. The wider you make the 'v', the more ploughing the ski will do. You will learn to regulate your speed very effectively by adjusting your plough, but a sound piece of advice is to use the snowplough before you need it. You will probably see skiers putting their left foot out of the ruts for stability at higher speeds, without necessarily using a plough at all.

Two ski snowplough

The ruts are quite often completely missing on steep hills. Everyone has to resort to herringbone for going up and a two-ski snowplough for down. The snow is likely to be very smooth, so you will need the biggest, widest plough you can muster.

Using both skis in a plough is a natural progression from one. Start down your practice hill with your skis side by side on the flat snow between the sets of ruts. After a couple of metres, slowly spread both skis evenly while turning your feet in at the same time. The skis will move sideways easily and freely when you are on the move, so don't do anything violent. Both skis should be evenly weighted at all times, and tilted onto their inside edges. It is tempting to let your legs straighten when making a wide plough, but if you can sit a bit so that your legs can stay flexed, you will have a better feel for what is going on. Experiment with sizes of plough and the amount of tilt on your skis.

Your skis should be tilted onto their inside edges when snowploughing.

Turning

The snowplough is vital for speed control, and an added bonus is that we can also use it for changing direction. If a skier were to fall on a hill in front of you, it is convenient to be able to nip out of the ruts, plough around them in a graceful curve and re-enter the ruts further down.

Look for a slope with no hard lumps or ridges on it and start down with a comfortably wide snowplough. Both skis can be flat on the snow to allow them to run freely, but be aware that even small lumps can catch the outer edge of a ski and make it jerk. Keep exactly the same size of plough and exactly the same goalkeeper position throughout the whole exercise. The only thing you have to do is to turn both feet gently but firmly in the direction you wish to go. There will be a delay from when you send the 'turn please' message through your feet, to the skis. For an awful moment you might be tempted to take extreme action, but don't do anything, just gently rotate the feet and wait. A bystander should not see any evidence that you are about to turn, in other words use the feet only, not the shoulders or hips or anything else. Be sure you keep the snowplough shape with the tips close but not touching; if you lose the plough you lose control. As soon as you feel your skis beginning to turn, take the pressure off and smoothly apply the same gentle twisting of the feet to turn in the opposite direction. Your skis will snake their way down leaving a series of gentle arcs in the snow. Keep the turns very small to begin with, hardly changing direction.

These turns are fine for delicate manoeuvres at low speeds, but we need something more powerful for negotiating bends on a long hill. Suppose we intend to make a sharp turn to the right. The body position is as before, but now we need to apply extra pressure through the left ski into the snow. The automatic reaction when intending to turn to the right, is to lean in that direction. Unfortunately that doesn't work on skis, you actually need to think of the lower ski, in this case the left ski, as the power ski and learn to trust it. You will not be able to put any real pressure on that ski if you are leaning away from it. If we tilt that ski onto it's edge at the same time, it will bite and turn more effectively. The right ski can lie flat on the snow and should be, in effect, the passenger. It's main function being to help with retaining the 'v' formation, otherwise to stay out of the way. When you need to press hard onto a ski, you might be tempted to move the whole body onto it and straighten that leg to make it feel stronger. You will get lots of pressure, but the ski will now be flat and can therefore catch the wrong edge, so it could stop suddenly, or get kicked across the other one. Always keep your upper body centrally between the skis, applying pressure through the whole foot both down and away from you at the same time. This is not particularly comfortable, but try to keep the upper body relaxed and the legs well flexed. When you learn to keep a ski on it's edge when turning, you will have excellent control over both direction and speed.

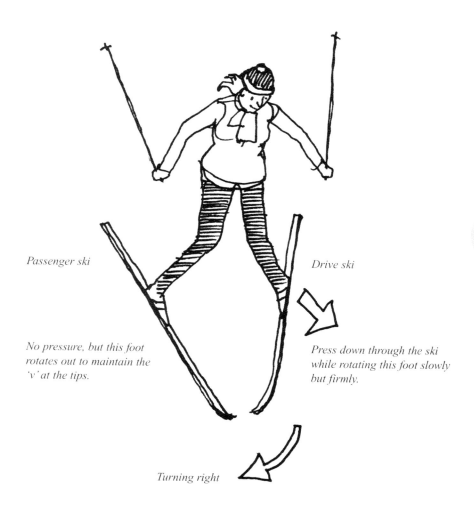

Passenger ski

Drive ski

No pressure, but this foot rotates out to maintain the 'v' at the tips.

Press down through the ski while rotating this foot slowly but firmly.

Turning right

Diagonal gait

This unlikely name describes that flowing graceful action of a skier at speed. If done efficiently, one could cover huge distances with no more effort than would be required by a gentle jog. You could think of diagonal gait as a kind of slow motion jog. The slow motion element is to allow time for the skier to stand over the front ski while it glides for a moment. The glide is produced by launching yourself up and forward, on to each ski in turn, with a bit of umph, then standing on each ski until it runs out of momentum. Combine this with a long firm pull with the poles, used alternately in harmony with the legs, and you will gain considerably more distance, per stride, than you would by walking. As your technique improves, you will require fewer strides per hundred meters. It is all about eating up distance while maintaining a sustainable rhythm. If you can't hold a conversation with a fellow skier while moving along, then you are working too hard. If you intend to ski for several hours, you need to be economical with your energy. It takes an extreme level of fitness to be able to run on skis hour after hour. A reasonable target for someone who has done one week of skiing is about 15km in one day. That should take about 4-5hrs. using a mixture of walking, jogging and resting.

The back of the ski can leave the snow with a longer stride.

Getting the penny to drop

Some people are lucky or gifted or whatever, and they start performing the diagonal gait after only a brief explanation and demonstration. Others have no desire to try more than a gentle walk. Everyone else falls somewhere between. There is nothing clever about diagonal gait, it is simply a co-ordination thing. Once you have understood the physical movements required, it is only practice to let the body learn the precise timing and feel. For those who like to grapple with the theory, here is the reasoning: if you are standing still and press one foot straight down, you will achieve excellent stick but no forward momentum. If you press straight back, on the other hand, the ski will simply shoot backwards because you had no platform from which to thrust forward. It follows then that a combination of downward pressure combined with some kicking action is the best way to gain forward movement. On any given snow with any given wax, there will be an optimum angle between up and forward thrust to produce the most glide. The better the skier, the lower the angle he manages to kick from, so the more forward thrust he creates for every stride. Here are three tried and tested ways to help you crack this particular nut.

Low to high

Find a flat track, and stand with your feet side by side in the ruts. You will not need your poles for now, so take them off and hold them half way along. Start with both knees well bent and press one ski firmly into the snow to create a platform from which you can leap up and forward onto the other ski. You are going from a crouched position at the moment of press to a higher position when balancing over the front ski. You might well feel unstable while gliding on the front ski, but if you commit all your weight to it and do your best to stand centrally with the leg a little flexed, it will get easier. Just before the front ski runs out of glide, bring the back foot up level once more, bend both knees deeply and repeat the sequence using the other leg. Both skis should stay on the snow throughout, but even so, this is a very mechanical way to learn and it is not easy to be smooth. The real benefit of this drill is that one learns to start low and finish high – which is the opposite of what you do when walking.

Jogging

Start as with the previous drill, without poles. Begin by jogging on the spot, but with your skis always in contact with the snow. Your head should be bobbing up and down as you bounce off alternate feet. At the moment you have lots of stick, but no forward drive. Keep the jogging going while you slide the skis forward, beginning to exaggerate the knee bend at the moment of press, then standing on the front ski longer. Think of it as trying to run in deep water, all your actions become bigger and slower. You might well find it helpful to swing your arms quite aggressively, pointing at each leading ski tip with the opposite hand to keep synchronisation. When you get going, you will need to swing your arms in a long arc, keeping them almost straight and sweeping them past your thighs on the way back and through. Try for a smooth rhythm, with only a small jerk as you bounce forward off each ski. As your balance and timing improve, you will need to use less and less muscle power.

Skating

Perhaps the simplest introduction to diagonal gait is to think of it as speed skating, but in a straight line. The long glide after an explosive thrust is common to both, resulting in that deceptive slow motion look to the rhythm. Even the long arm swings have much in common, but you don't have to bend over double or wear the skin-tight plastic bag that they pour themselves into. Instead of progressing in a zigzag, lifting each skate, we move in a straight line, with our 'skates' on the snow. Try to imagine the flowing rhythm of the skater then just do it in a straight line with a bit of extra bounce. It really is as simple as that.

Double poling

Strong skiers will often give their legs a rest by propelling themselves along for considerable distances with only their poles. If the ruts even on the flat are very slippery, this technique is actually faster than diagonal gait. Newcomers to the sport tend to double pole down hills that are not quite steep enough for the skis to move on their own, but where walking feels unstable. The poles are used simultaneously in a series of long powerful thrusts, taking advantage of the weight of the body to reduce strain on the arms.

Stand with your skis side-by-side and lean forward with your whole body fully extended while you plant both poles a few inches in front of your feet. Your arms should be reasonably bent, so that you can immediately lean down with your upper body, putting pressure on the poles from above. That action will make you slide forward, and if you also pull down with your stomach muscles, you will slide well past your poles. At the point when you are almost bent double, your hands will be close to your thighs. Now is the time to use arm power and not before. Push the poles hard, all the way back, until your arms are fully extended. You will need to let go of the handles completely to do this properly, neatly picking up the poles again between finger and thumb on the way forward. Stand up straight again and then bring the poles up once more to repeat the sequence. Work on the concept that the body does the first half of the work and the arms finish off.

Classic or skating

These are two distinct forms of x-country skiing. Each has it's own techniques and equipment, even their own type of track. Skating on skis became possible with the introduction of track grooming. Classic skiing was kept pure by creating a separate discipline and forbidding the use of skating except to change tracks. Skating is faster and more physically demanding. Shorter, stiffer skis are used, with glide wax under the entire length, boots have more ankle support and the poles are longer. The vast majority of recreational skiers never skate because the technique takes a long time to master, and it is not possible to drift along side by side chatting and enjoying the scenery, because each skier needs to use the full width of the track. Skating is best suited to fitness freaks and endurance athletes.

Touring

As the word implies, this sport involves travelling long distances, often over untracked snow, and can include staying overnight in mountain huts or snow holes. The backpack can be quite heavy, so the skis tend to be wider and stronger to stop the skier sinking in too far. The boots are traditionally leather and the poles often adjustable, to cope with differing terrain. Metal edged skis help with grip, and 'skins' are stuck to the ski base to allow a skier to walk straight up even steep hills. Telemark turns, with one foot behind the other, are the recommended turns for deep snow when you have no heel binding. Obviously, you need to be quite competent to consider going on a tour, but the experience is always unforgettable. A comprehensive hut-to-hut system now exists in several countries, with maps and information readily available to the general public. In Norway, you would contact DNT, Den Norske Turistforening, who have over 400 cabins, some of which are permanently manned. This would be the ultimate 'get away from it all' holiday, a type of holiday that is becoming increasingly hard to find, but will always remain the realm of the relatively intrepid.

Signing off

This book barely scratches the surface of what there is to discover about walking on snow, but it will give you a sound start. I hope that you will enjoy many exhilarating trips into the world's winter wonderlands, taking away with you powerful memories, leaving behind only your tracks.

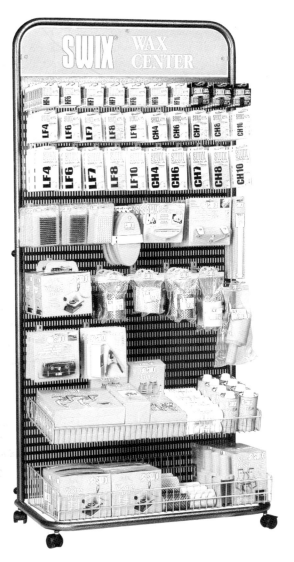

skiiers stick with swix
www.swix.no